DO YOU BELIEVE?
LOCH NESS MONSTER

by Natalie Deniston

pogo

Ideas for Parents and Teachers

Pogo Books let children practice reading informational text while introducing them to nonfiction features such as headings, labels, sidebars, maps, and diagrams, as well as a table of contents, glossary, and index.

Carefully leveled text with a strong photo match offers early fluent readers the support they need to succeed.

Before Reading

- "Walk" through the book and point out the various nonfiction features. Ask the student what purpose each feature serves.
- Look at the glossary together. Read and discuss the words.

Read the Book

- Have the child read the book independently.
- Invite him or her to list questions that arise from reading.

After Reading

- Discuss the child's questions. Talk about how he or she might find answers to those questions.
- Prompt the child to think more. Ask: Do you believe there is a creature in Loch Ness?

Pogo Books are published by Jump!
5357 Penn Avenue South
Minneapolis, MN 55419
www.jumplibrary.com

Copyright © 2025 Jump!
International copyright reserved in all countries. No part of this book may be reproduced in any form without written permission from the publisher.

Library of Congress Cataloging-in-Publication Data

Names: Deniston, Natalie, author.
Title: Loch Ness monster / by Natalie Deniston.
Description: Minneapolis, MN: Jump!, Inc., [2025]
Series: Do you believe? | Includes index.
Audience: Ages 7–10
Identifiers: LCCN 2023057543 (print)
LCCN 2023057544 (ebook)
ISBN 9798892132275 (hardcover)
ISBN 9798892132282 (paperback)
ISBN 9798892132299 (ebook)
Subjects: LCSH: Loch Ness monster–Juvenile literature.
Monsters–Scotland–Juvenile literature.
Classification: LCC QL89.2.L6 D486 2025 (print)
LCC QL89.2.L6 (ebook)
DDC 001.944–dc23/eng/20240205
LC record available at https://lccn.loc.gov/2023057543
LC ebook record available at https://lccn.loc.gov/2023057544

Editor: Jenna Gleisner
Designer: Emma Almgren-Bersie

Photo Credits: Lensalot/iStock, cover (background); Matt84/iStock, cover (monster); gremlin/iStock, 1; Jeff Morin/Shutterstock, 3; aluxum/iStock, 4; ClaraRguez/iStock, 5; Daniel Eskridge/Shutterstock, 6-7 (monster); 13threephotography/iStock, 6-7 (background); sunlow/iStock, 8; David Lyons/Alamy, 9; AlfvanBeem/Wikimedia, 10; 7exxe7/iStock, 10-11; Carlos G. Lopez/Shutterstock, 12-13; Chronicle/Alamy, 14-15; Kit Leong/Shutterstock, 16; dpa picture alliance/Alamy, 17; Dotted Yeti/Shutterstock, 18-19; Sergii Figurnyi/Shutterstock, 20-21; Dana Kenedy/Dreamstime, 23.

Printed in the United States of America at Corporate Graphics in North Mankato, Minnesota.

TABLE OF CONTENTS

CHAPTER 1
Welcome to Loch Ness! 4

CHAPTER 2
Meet the Monster 8

CHAPTER 3
Nessie Today 16

QUICK FACTS & TOOLS
Timeline 22
Glossary 23
Index 24
To Learn More 24

CHAPTER 1
WELCOME TO LOCH NESS!

In Scotland, there is a lake called Loch Ness. The word "loch" comes from the Gaelic word for "lake."

Loch Ness

Loch Ness is more than 23 miles (37 kilometers) long. It is more than 750 feet (229 meters) deep. The water is dark. It is hard to see. Some people believe this place is home to a monster!

The Loch Ness monster is also called Nessie. Nessie is believed to be nearly 20 feet (6.1 m) long. It swims with **flippers**. Some people also think it has a long neck and tail.

flipper

CHAPTER 1

TAKE A LOOK!

Where is Loch Ness? Take a look!

CHAPTER 2
MEET THE MONSTER

Nobody knows if Nessie is real. But some people search for it. They believe the stories. Where do the stories come from?

More than 1,500 years ago, the Pict people lived in Scotland. They **carved** stone. Many Pict carvings still exist. Some show a mysterious creature. Some people believe it is an **aquatic** monster.

Pict carving

CHAPTER 2

The earliest written story of Nessie involves **Saint** Columba. In the year 565, Columba saw a monster in River Ness. It was about to attack a swimmer. Columba told the monster to leave. It went into Loch Ness. The swimmer was saved.

Saint Columba

CHAPTER 2

River Ness

CHAPTER 2

In 1933, a couple drove by Loch Ness. They said a monster splashed in the water. Their story brought visitors to their hotel on Loch Ness.

Later that year, a newspaper hired Marmaduke Wetherell. Why? He was asked to find the monster. He said he found strange **tracks**. He made **casts** of the tracks. Experts looked at them. Were they from Nessie? No. They were fake.

WHAT DO YOU THINK?

Wetherell faked **evidence** of the Loch Ness monster. Why might someone do this?

Robert Wilson came forward in 1934. He said he took a photo of the monster. The photo became famous. People believed it was proof of Nessie!

But in 1994, it was revealed the photo wasn't of Nessie. It was of a **model** made to look like the monster. It was made from a toy submarine.

DID YOU KNOW?

Wetherell took the photograph. Why? He was mad people from the newspaper figured out his tracks were fake. He wanted to fool them.

CHAPTER 3
NESSIE TODAY

In 1973, a man named Adrian Shine started the Loch Ness Project. This group runs the Loch Ness Centre. Members look for Nessie.

People take boats onto the water. Some use **sonar** to search for Nessie.

CHAPTER 3

What could Nessie be? There are many **theories**. One says Nessie is a plesiosaur. These were large reptiles. They lived in water.

Another theory says Nessie is a large fish. Eels live in Loch Ness. Maybe Nessie is a giant eel.

DID YOU KNOW?

Plesiosaurs lived during the time of the dinosaurs. They went **extinct** at the same time. When? Nearly 66 million years ago!

CHAPTER 3

In August 2023, the Loch Ness Centre held another search for Nessie. It used **drones**. It recorded sounds underwater. Hundreds of people joined. But they didn't find Nessie. Do you think there is a monster in Loch Ness?

WHAT DO YOU THINK?

Most evidence of the Loch Ness monster is fake. Why do you think so many people still look for Nessie?

CHAPTER 3

QUICK FACTS & TOOLS

TIMELINE

People have told stories of a monster in Loch Ness for more than 1,000 years. Take a look!

300-900
The Picts of Scotland make carvings of a creature similar to the Loch Ness monster.

565
Saint Columba is said to have saved a swimmer from a monster near Loch Ness.

APRIL 1933
A couple driving along Loch Ness reports a monster in the water.

DECEMBER 1933
Marmaduke Wetherell fakes monster tracks.

APRIL 1934
Robert Wilson claims he photographed the monster.

1973
Adrian Shine starts the Loch Ness Project. The group searches for the monster.

AUGUST 26-27, 2023
The Loch Ness Centre hosts a monster hunt. Nothing is found.

22 QUICK FACTS & TOOLS

GLOSSARY

aquatic: Living in water.

carved: Cut pieces of wood, stone, or other hard substances into particular shapes.

casts: Objects made by pouring liquid, such as plaster, into molds and letting them harden.

drones: Aircraft without pilots that are controlled remotely.

evidence: Information that proves if something is true.

extinct: No longer found alive and known about only through fossils or history.

flippers: Broad, flat limbs used for swimming.

model: A thing built as an example to show how something larger will look.

saint: A person who has been officially recognized by Christian churches for living a very holy life.

sonar: A machine used on ships and submarines that sends out underwater sound waves to find objects.

theories: Ideas or opinions that are based on some facts or evidence but are not proven.

tracks: Marks left behind by a moving animal or person.

INDEX

carvings 9
casts 13
drones 21
eels 18
flippers 6
Loch Ness Centre 16, 21
model 14
neck 6
photo 14
Pict people 9
plesiosaur 18
River Ness 7, 10
Saint Columba 10
Shine, Adrian 16
sonar 17
stories 8, 10, 13
tail 6
theories 18
tracks 13, 14
water 5, 13, 17, 18, 21
Wetherell, Marmaduke 13, 14
Wilson, Robert 14

TO LEARN MORE

Finding more information is as easy as 1, 2, 3.
1. Go to www.factsurfer.com
2. Enter "LochNessmonster" into the search box.
3. Choose your book to see a list of websites.